SLIM CHANCE

SLIM CHANCE

by Peter Gordon

JOSEF WEINBERGER PLAYS

LONDON

SLIM CHANCE
First published in 2007
by Josef Weinberger Ltd
12-14 Mortimer Street, London, W1T 3JJ
www.josef-weinberger.com general.info@jwmail.co.uk

ISBN 10: 0 85676 305 5
ISBN 13: 978 0 85676 305 2

Printed by Biddles Ltd, King's Lynn, Norfolk

CHARACTERS

JEAN

BETTY

IRENE

ANNE

DEBBIE

MARJORIE

EDNA

LOUISE

The action of the play takes place in a room in a church hall in the present day.

A room in a Church Hall. The set may be as simple or elaborate as desired. One entrance/exit is required. A stack of eight chairs and a small table are upstage, together with several cardboard boxes. One of the boxes contains several stage props, including a cardboard cut-out skull. Additional items of furniture and notices including a "No Smoking" sign are scattered around to give the impression of a well-used hall.

JEAN *is pacing around the room impatiently, looking frequently at her watch and muttering to herself. She is in her mid-forties and smartly, though conservatively, dressed. Her shopping bag, containing bathroom scales, portable CD player, folders and handbook, is on the floor, down left.*

JEAN (*muttering to herself*) Why do I bother? No appreciation. No, "well done, Jean" . . . no support. One does one's best but . . . (*Checking her watch again.*) why does one bother!

(BETTY *enters, closely followed by* ANNE *and* IRENE. BETTY *is in her mid-forties and well-dressed.* ANNE *is in her early thirties and is casually dressed.* IRENE, *also casually dressed, is aged about forty and is something of a rebel. They all wear coats.*)

BETTY (*cheerfully, as she enters*) Hello, Jean.

JEAN (*frosty, checking her watch again pointedly*) Good evening.

BETTY Bit frosty out there tonight.

JEAN Really wouldn't know, dear. I've been in here an eternity . . . waiting.

IRENE (*quietly to* ANNE) Bit frosty in here as well!

JEAN (*letting the matter drop and looking at her watch again*) Ten past seven. Really is too much, you know. Week in, week out!

IRENE At least we're consistent.

ANNE Anyway, you never get going 'til at least twenty past.

JEAN (*increasingly frustrated*) I can't start when I'm the only one here! Frightfully difficult to organize anything efficiently when unreliability is rampant!

IRENE But it's human nature to be unreliable . . . it's a design fault.

BETTY People only come late because you let them get away with it. If you started dead on time, we'd all get here. We'd be frightened we missed something.

IRENE Perhaps you've finally done it, Jean. They've all lost so much weight they've slipped down a grate on the way here. They'll all be sitting in a manhole wishing they'd never joined a slimming club!

(IRENE *pulls a packet of cigarettes from her bag.*)

JEAN Unlikely on past performance. (*Noticing* IRENE'S *cigarettes.*) That's not allowed, Irene, as you well know.

(JEAN *points triumphantly at the "No smoking" sign.*)

JEAN Pulbic place. The hall is now a smokeless zone. Quite rightly in my opinion.

IRENE (*outraged*) But what about *my* human rights? I demand to smoke wherever I want.

JEAN In this case your rights take second place to social awareness and conscience, dear. Smokers are the minority and must yield to the majority who do not wish to be asphyxiated . . . ergo, smoking is no-go.

IRENE What does all that mean in English!

JEAN It means put them away, dear. Thank you so much.

IRENE It's outrageous! Some people have nothing better to do than meddle in other peoples lives! Smoking is my one remaining pleasure.

BETTY And eating.

IRENE Alright, one of my *two* remaining pleasures. (ANNE *raises her eyebrows. Reluctantly,* IRENE *returns the cigarettes to her handbag.*) Okay, so there may be others but I'm not prepared to go in to detail. (*Defiant.*) I may rebel later . . . I may need one when I've been weighed.

JEAN (*resigned*) That would not surprise me in the least, Irene.

IRENE (*trying to sound convincing*) I've stuck to the diet!

(ANNE *desperately tries to control a snigger.*)

(*indignant*) I have! (*Defensive.*) I've got big bones.

ANNE And they get bigger by the day!

JEAN Less bickering, girls, please. Let's assemble the chairs or we'll never get started. Anne, would you give me a hand with the table, dear? Thank you so much.

(*During the course of the following conversation,* JEAN *and* ANNE *carry the table down left.* IRENE *and* BETTY *arrange six chairs in a rough semi-circle, stretching from centre stage, down right. An additional chair is placed by the table.*)

(*gloomy*) I feel I should inform you that another letter has winged its way from head office. Not good.

ANNE What's it got to do with them? We pay our subs!

JEAN Anne, dear . . . this is supposed to be a slimming club. A collective massive weight gain has *everything* to do with them. They formulate the diet sheets, the slimming aids . . . they feel that it reflects badly on them . . . they could be seen as responsible.

IRENE (*laughing*) I can just see it on the news . . . (*Imitating a newsreader.*) "Earlier today, a member of a slimming club spontaneously exploded. Directors of the club are expected to face corporate manslaughter charges."

ANNE — Who cares? The directors are probably a load of old men who are just after a fat profit.

IRENE — An unfortunate turn of phrase . . . *fat* profit.

JEAN — I fail to see any reason for levity! I'm the group leader . . . ill-informed people might believe that your abysmal performance reflects badly on me. A preposterous idea of course.

BETTY — We all have our cross to bear, Jean.

JEAN — But I am endeavouring to make all of yours lighter!

(*The table and chairs should now be in position.* JEAN *starts to organize her things on the table. She is very precise about the exact positioning of things on the table.* IRENE *wanders over to the cardboard boxes.*)

IRENE — What's this then . . . jumble sale? The WI are murder with them you know. Last time, I stood still for five seconds and they sold me to a sad old man in bicycle clips. I don't know how he was going to get me home!

JEAN — Don't meddle, dear . . . thank you so much. They're props for my thespian society.

IRENE — What are you practicing for this time?

JEAN — Thespians do not practice, Irene . . . they rehearse. We're doing a little Halloween entertainment for the over-eighties activities group.

IRENE They'll find it a break from hang gliding I suppose. (*Picking the cardboard cut-out skull from one of the boxes.*) Alas, poor Eric . . . I knew him well.

JEAN (*sighing*) Yorrick, dear.

IRENE (*winking at the others*) Nope, this one's Eric . . . founder member of the Slimming club . . . see what happens when you get too far under your target weight! (*Tossing the skull back into the box.*) I think I'd be good at drama.

ANNE You'd never stick to the script.

IRENE I quite fancy myself as a leading lady . . . all hair lacquer and heaving bosoms.

(JEAN *returns to sorting things on the table. She is not quite certain as to the exact positioning of pens and pencils and keeps changing them around.* DEBBIE *enters nonchalantly. She is younger than the rest and is dressed casually but fashionably.*)

DEBBIE Hi.

JEAN (*looking pointedly at her watch*) Good evening. Miss your bus?

DEBBIE No, they're very hard to miss . . . especially those new big bendy ones! (*Innocent.*) Did you miss yours? You want to get your eyes checked.

JEAN It is sixteen minutes past, Debbie . . . we commence at seven.

DEBBIE No we don't. We usually commence at about twenty past.

IRENE When you've finally arranged your pens properly.

JEAN We commence . . . *I* commence, at seven. Be more prompt next week, Debbie, please, thank you so much.

DEBBIE (*disinterested*) Yeah, whatever. By the way, Tracy's not coming any more. Not for about seven and a half months anyway!

JEAN Pregnant again! How could she?

IRENE I'll explain later, Jean . . . I don't think now's the time.

JEAN But she promised faithfully that she was going to attend regularly. How can I run a group on this basis! I'm trying to build numbers up.

BETTY So's Tracy by the sound of it. She's only just had the last one.

IRENE Maybe she'll stop when she finds out what's causing it. Look on the bright side, Jean . . . it might explain some of the weight she's put on.

JEAN (*brightening*) Might it? Yes . . . quite. Good point, dear . . . well done.

(JEAN *pulls a sheet of paper from one of her folders and makes a note.*)

ANNE Didn't she use one of those birthing pools last time?

DEBBIE Yeah. Never again though.

ANNE Oh? I thought that they were supposed to be very good.

DEBBIE Oh, it worked brilliantly for her and the baby. It's just her husband. Stupid man fainted and fell in at the vital moment and had to be resuscitated. (*Placing her coat on the back of a chair.*) Anybody know who that is hanging around outside?

JEAN What! Outside here?

DEBBIE Well, if I meant outside the town hall I wouldn't be mentioning it would I?

JEAN Didn't you ask her what she wanted?

DEBBIE She looked as though she *wanted* to run away. If I'd spoken to her, I think she would have.

JEAN (*sighing*) So it's up to me is it? (*Moving to the door.*) Why is it that it seems to fall to my lot to organize everything?

IRENE Because the verb 'organize' is associated with the noun 'organizer', which is what you officially are.

JEAN I never realized you had such a keen grasp of the English language, Irene! Thank you so much.

(JEAN *exits.*)

IRENE The strain of top management.

BETTY So what do you think . . . new recruit? I know it's sadistic but I love seeing their faces when they get their first look at the diet sheets . . . it's the frantic staring eyes that I so enjoy.

IRENE I need someone very large to join . . . to make me look good. Somebody shaped like a weather balloon would do.

DEBBIE Well, this one's skinny as anything. I'd say she needs to put weight on!

BETTY She's come to the right place then. We've got a long and successful history of fattening people up!

IRENE Excuse me! (*Proudly.*) I've lost weight consistently since I joined.

ANNE But you keep putting it back on again.

IRENE Picky!

ANNE So what's the point?

IRENE There's every point! If I hadn't been losing weight in between all the times I've been putting it on, I'd be much heavier now than when I started. As it is, I'm only marginally heavier.

(*The others look at her disapprovingly.*)

Well, I'm not a saint you know!

DEBBIE We'd noticed. (*Sitting and reaching for her bag.*) Anybody want a ciggy?

IRENE Not allowed . . . Miss says so.

(*During the following conversation,* ANNE *wanders over to the desk and tries to look at the details in* JEAN'S *folders.*)

DEBBIE Oh . . . right. Wayne thinks I've given up . . . silly sod. We've got a bet on. I caught him smoking in the meter cupboard the other day . . . claimed he was checking for gas leaks. That little mistake cost him a fiver.

IRENE I've been giving up for over fifteen months you know. I go to classes on Thursdays.

BETTY It doesn't seem to be working too well.

IRENE There's some smashing fellers go there though. All twitchy with withdrawal symptoms and just dying to do something with their hands.

ANNE What is it with you? I don't know why you've got this thing about men.

BETTY They're not all like yours was, Anne. You can't tar them all with the same brush.

ANNE Just watch me!

IRENE You want to watch yourself if you ask me. If Jean catches you looking through her files . . . !

ANNE I can handle Jean.

(JEAN *enters briskly.* ANNE *hurriedly drops the folders and tries to look casual, leaning against the table.* JEAN *suspects her and scowls.* ANNE *creeps away to a chair to the amusement of the others.* LOUISE *follows* JEAN *into the room. She is aged about thirty, dressed very plainly and is painfully shy which shows in her every action.*)

JEAN Attention please, girls. I'd like you all to meet our very special new member. Now then, Louise, we've got Betty, Irene, Debbie and (*Scowling.*) Anne . . . who I suspect was being just a little bit naughty when we came in.

IRENE (*in mock seriousness*) Yes, she was, Miss.

JEAN Still, we don't let that worry us do we?

IRENE No, Miss.

JEAN It's funny you know, Louise . . . (*Making her joke very condescendingly.*) one would normally regard us as one *big* happy family but in the circumstances I like to think of us as one *little* happy family.

LOUISE (*flatly*) Oh.

JEAN Just a slimming club joke, dear . . . *little* family.

LOUISE Oh.

JEAN Still, you don't have to find it amusing . . . not compulsory. Right . . . shall we get on then? Thank you so much.

BETTY Been in the area long, Louise?

LOUISE (*nervously*) Quite a long time, yes (*Pause while she thinks.*) . . . *always*, actually. I tend not to get out much . . . through choice . . . nobody makes me stay in . . . I just do.

IRENE Well don't worry, Louise, you're safe with us. We won't eat you . . . practically anything else we can get our hands on, yes, but we've avoided cannibalism so far.

LOUISE Oh.

IRENE Another of our little slimming club jokes.

LOUISE Oh . . . oh yes. (*Now feeling ultra-sensitive, she lets out a long shrill uneasy laugh.*)

DEBBIE Are you sure you've come to the right place, Louise? You don't look as though you need to lose an ounce.

LOUISE Oh I do. I know I do. My husband . . . that's Malcolm . . . he thought I ought to diet.

ANNE (*outraged*) You mean you came here just to please him? You want to go straight home and tell him to stick his diet up his a–

JEAN (*interrupting quickly*) . . . Anne, dear . . . that's quite enough, thank you.

LOUISE Oh, no, Malcolm's right. (*Uncertain.*) My Malcolm's always right . . . he's a dentist.

JEAN Well, we'll weigh you later, dear, then we'll know exactly where we stand.

(MARJORIE *and* EDNA *enter and make their way straight across stage, talking as they go. They are both much older than the rest, and talk with broader accents.* EDNA *has the annoying habit of repeating odd words from other people's sentences.*)

MARJ — Evening all. It was all my fault . . . sorry we're late.

EDNA — We're late.

JEAN — I do wish that . . .

EDNA — It wasn't entirely your fault, Marj! Your Arthur's more like.

JEAN — It makes things very . . .

MARJ — No, Edna, fair play. 'E 'ad cause. If I 'adn't got meself in such a mess with meself, 'e wouldn't 'ave 'ad cause.

EDNA — She was in a right mess with 'erself.

JEAN — If we could possibly just . . .

EDNA — But it weren't your fault you got in a mess! Anyone would 'ave.

JEAN } — (*shouting*) Ladies, if we could please just . . .

MARJ } — Well, no . . . I'll give you that, but what . . . (*Realizing that* JEAN *is speaking.*) Sorry, Mrs L, were you saying something, love?

EDNA — Saying something.

JEAN Thank you, Marjorie. Simply trying to make a point vis-à-vis lateness. More effort next week perhaps? Thank you so much. If we could forge ahead?

MARJ Forge away, love. Don't let us stop you.

EDNA Forge away.

JEAN Thank you so much.

(JEAN *pauses for breath, opens her mouth to speak, but is cut off by* MARJ *talking to the others.*)

MARJ 'Ere, what a day I've 'ad. Talk about calamities, I've 'ad 'em all.

EDNA Calamities. 'Er cat's poorly. It drank 'alf a pint o' paint.

(JEAN *looks heavenward in despair and slumps into the chair behind the table with a resigned expression on her face. She buries her head in her hands. The others also gradually sit, failing to notice that* LOUISE *is left standing with no chair.* LOUISE *looks around anxiously wondering what to do.*)

MARJ See, I'd just started on our back room . . . 'ere, you should 'ave seen the state of the walls.

EDNA Back room.

MARJ Anyway, I'd just popped out for a second . . .

EDNA Popped out.

MARJ ... to catch the window cleaner ... very nice young man.

EDNA Nice young man. And when she came back, there 'e was, all covered in paint.

MARJ The cat of course ... not the window cleaner. There he was ... just sitting there ... with turquoise paint all over 'is 'ed.

EDNA 'Is 'ed. Dripping on the carpet.

MARJ It used to be a lovely carpet as well, didn't it, Ed? I think you were with me when I got it.

EDNA That's right. Mind you, that's going back a bit. Just before my Eric went in for 'is op.

MARJ That's it. Ooh, he was terribly sore wasn't he!

EDNA Terribly sore. Two months before 'e could get 'is legs back together!

MARJ Anyway, when Arthur got 'ome, 'e was livid. Threatened to chuck the cat in the river.

EDNA In the river. (*Sadly.*) It'll never be the same again. Like my Eric.

MARJ Oh, he calmed down a bit. He didn't throw 'im in.

EDNA No, your carpet. Marj, not your cat.

MARJ (*philosophically*) Well, I've done my best with it. I'll just 'ave to see 'ow it dries. I could always put a rug over the turquoise I suppose. (*Noticing* JEAN *with her head in her hands.*)

'Ere are you all right, Mrs L? 'Aven't got an 'eadache 'ave you?

JEAN (*in despair*) I wonder if we might just get on, please?

MARJ (*concerned*) As long as your up to it, love. You want to be careful. (*To* EDNA.) My sister's brain 'aemorrhoid started just like that!

EDNA Just like that.

JEAN We'll start with . . . (*Noticing that* LOUISE *is standing.*) Why are you standing, dear?

LOUISE (*embarrassed*) Because I wanted to . . . well, there wasn't a . . . (*She points vaguely at the chairs.*)

BETTY (*realizing* LOUISE's *plight*) You need a chair, Louise. I'll get you one.

EDNA A chair.

(*As* LOUISE *hops apologetically from one foot to the other,* BETTY *fetches the last chair from the stack and puts it down for her.* LOUISE *sits.*)

JEAN We always start with a few simple exercises, Louise, to help us tone all our important little muscles.

LOUISE Oh . . . sorry.

(LOUISE *stands as she expects it is required.*)

JEAN (*consulting her notes*) We'll make a start then shall we. Now the first one . . . (*Looking up and noticing* LOUISE.) . . . you're standing again, dear. Would you like the little girl's room?

MARJ Just down the corridor.

LOUISE Oh, no . . . I wasn't . . . I thought . . . with the exercises? (*Deciding that to play along is the easiest way out.*) Thank you. (LOUISE *smiles in embarrassment as she makes her way to the door.*) I won't be a moment . . . sorry . . . sorry.

EDNA I'll need it meself in a minute.

(LOUISE'S *nerve breaks and she bolts the final few steps to the door and exits rapidly.*)

JEAN (*calling after her*) Just join in when you get back, dear. (*To the others.*) Ready then, girls. Let's give it everything we've got.

(JEAN *switches the CD player on and some music starts. A very slow, well known, sing-along type tune.*)

(*just before the music starts, very quickly*) A one, a two, a one two three four . . . (*The music starts very slowly.*) Off we go then . . . neck movements, side to side . . . a left and right and left and right . . .

(*They all sit in front of* JEAN *as she directs them, slowly tilting their heads from side to side.* BETTY *has no sense of timing and tends to move her head at random whilst anxiously watching to see how the others are doing it.*)

Come along, Debbie . . . a little enthusiasm into it, please!

DEBBIE Enthusiasm! How is anybody supposed to get enthusiastic about this!

EDNA I think it's very restful.

DEBBIE It's not supposed to be restful!

JEAN And left and right and left . . . left . . . left. Keep in time with the music, Betty . . . thank you so much. And left and right and left and right.

(MARJ *and* EDNA *start to sing along to the music, slowly swaying together.*)

IRENE What a row! Have you heard yourselves!

JEAN And left and right. Betty, do try, dear. Marjorie, no singing, please . . . we're not licensed for singing.

(MARJ *and* EDNA *ignore her, lost in their own world.*)

(*louder*) Marjorie . . . quiet, please. Marjorie! (*With a grimace of resignation.*) Let's all sing along then . . . feel those muscles really working.

(*After a few seconds,* DEBBIE *leaps to her feet in frustration.*)

DEBBIE This is useless! Just look at you all!

JEAN It's very good for the neck, dear. Releases tension and I'm sure it's very slimming.

DEBBIE It's my legs that are too big . . . not my neck!

JEAN But we've got to be fair to everyone, Debbie. Some of us may have fat necks. Carry on girls. Left and right . . .

DEBBIE Oh, this is impossible.

(DEBBIE *storms over to the CD player and switches it off.*)

JEAN Debbie!

MARJ Oh, I was just enjoying that!

EDNA Enjoying that.

DEBBIE But it's not doing you any good! Can't you see that!

MARJ It's a nice sing-along though.

EDNA I enjoy a sing-along.

DEBBIE You shouldn't have enough breath to sing. We should be doing aerobics . . . then maybe we might get somewhere.

MARJ Oh, I don't think I want to be taking up aerobatics . . . not at my time of life.

EDNA No, we don't want to be going down that road.

DEBBIE (*taking a CD out of her handbag*) It's just a different kind of exercise . . . to get your cardiovascular system working.

JEAN — We are not going to be working anybody's cardiovascular system, thank you so much. It could damage us and I refuse to be held responsible. We must stick to the club's prescribed program.

ANNE — And since when has that done us any good!

IRENE — Exactly. (*Reaching out and taking the CD from* DEBBIE.) This is a democratic country and I have democratically decided that we don't want to do Missus Motivator's exercises any longer.

(IRENE *moves to the table and replaces* JEAN'S *CD with the new one.*)

JEAN — But it wasn't democratic. There are some of us against . . . aren't there girls?

IRENE — Oh, get a life, Jean.

(IRENE *switches on the CD which plays modern disco music.* DEBBIE *starts to gyrate around the room. The others watch, slightly mystified. As* DEBBIE *dances past the door she almost bumps into* LOUISE *who hesitantly enters the room. Before* LOUISE *has time to react,* DEBBIE *grabs her arm.*)

DEBBIE — Come on, Louise . . . aerobics . . . show them how to do it!

LOUISE — (*terrified*) But I can't . . .

DEBBIE — (*encouragingly*) Course you can!

(LOUISE *has little choice as* DEBBIE *forces her to dance alongside her. She encourages* LOUISE *to follow her own actions.* LOUISE *very self-consciously tries her best but whereas* DEBBIE *is graceful,* LOUISE *is clumsy and uncoordinated. One by one, the rest of them join in, with the exception of* JEAN *who stands watching furiously.*)

ANNE Come on, Jean . . . join in.

JEAN We don't have permission for disco dancing.

BETTY (*breathlessly*) It's rather good fun, actually. You want to give it a try, Jean.

(JEAN *looks away in disgust.*)

DEBBIE In a few minutes you'll really start to feel it doing you good?

EDNA It's ever so fast, isn't it?

(EDNA *and* MARJ *start to dance around each other and try to join in with the singing. All of the gyrations become gradually more frantic until suddenly* BETTY *shouts in pain and bends double, holding her back.*)

BETTY Aaagh . . . my back!

IRENE (*moving to her*) Are you all right, Betty? (JEAN *switches the music off with a self-satisfied and extravagant flourish.*)

BETTY It's my back. I can't move!

ANNE Get her onto this chair. Give me a hand.

(ANNE *and* IRENE *help* BETTY *into a chair.*)

BETTY Oh, thank you. I feel such a fool!

ANNE Is that any better now? How does it feel?

BETTY I'm sorry . . . just leave me. When I get my breath back it'll probably ease a bit.

JEAN (*with a superior expression*) Perhaps my advice was not so misplaced after all. Just a pity poor Betty has to suffer in order to demonstrate it. Some of you may feel that my methods are a little old fashioned, but they are tried and tested . . . the old ways are sometimes the best, Debbie.

DEBBIE It was only an accident. She could have twisted her neck with your stupid exercise!

JEAN (*smug*) I think not, Debbie . . . I think not.

MARJ (*helpfully, as she sits down*) I did a course in first aid once . . . run by St John it was. They didn't bother wi' backs though. You can't do much wi' backs. Wi' backs, once they're gone, they're gone.

EDNA (*thinking hard, sitting beside her*) Turps . . . that'd do the trick . . . turps.

MARJ Ooh, I doubt it Ed. I suppose you could try rubbing a bit in but St John never mentioned that one!

EDNA (*giggling*) No, your carpet! Not 'er back. Try turps on your carpet. You'd 'ave to be careful your dye didn't come out, mind.

MARJ — I could try it though, couldn't I? Anything's better than turquoise in the middle of 'yer floor! I've always said that.

EDNA — Always said that, yes.

JEAN — Excuse me, girls. If we could get back to the matter in hand!

(MARJ *and* EDNA *smile at* JEAN *innocently.*)

If sanity will prevail for a few moments I suggest we return to the original and approved programme of exercises?

DEBBIE — I still say they're too slow.

JEAN — But at least they haven't maimed anyone, dear.

ANNE — Come on, Jean! Betty wasn't used to it, that's all. If we did them regularly!

JEAN — And all end up as paraplegics! I think not. Right . . . necks at the ready, girls.

DEBBIE — No! You can't walk all over us like that! Let's take a vote on it . . .

ANNE — Yeah.

JEAN — Absolutely not.

MARJ — I don't mind 'aving a vote, do you Ed?

EDNA — No, I'm easy.

IRENE — (*chanting*) Vote, vote, vote, vote . . .

DEBBIE See.

JEAN (*sulking, with a heavy sigh*) Very well . . . as you force it upon me, I shall accede to your request . . .

EDNA Accede.

JEAN But I give notice that I will have to consider my position with this group very closely.

IRENE Can I be in charge when you've gone?

JEAN (*ignoring* IRENE) All those in favour of doing the sensible exercises recommended by the club, raise your hand.

(BETTY *is initially the only one to raise her hand.* MARJ *looks around and, seeing that only* BETTY'S *hand is raised, feels sorry for her and raises her own.*)

MARJ 'Ere 'ere.

EDNA (*seeing* MARJ *raise her hand, she also raises her own*) Aye.

JEAN That's three.

ANNE I thought you were enjoying the dancing, Marj!

MARJ Well I was, yes. But I like the other tune better . . . I know the words.

JEAN All those in favour of Debbie's outlandish routine which has crippled poor Betty . . . probably permanently.

(DEBBIE, ANNE *and* IRENE *raise their hands.*)

Three again.

IRENE You haven't voted, Louise.

LOUISE (*unhappily*) I don't really think I should. I've only just got here.

DEBBIE Come on, Louise, vote with us . . . you don't want to be sat here every week wobbling your head from side to side.

JEAN (*talking quickly*) Of course you do, dear. Anyway, you can't vote because you haven't officially joined yet. Casting vote is mine . . . I vote against. Shall we get on . . . no hard feelings?

DEBBIE That's not fair!

IRENE Fix, fix, fix . . .

JEAN I'm sorry, dear, but you were keen on the democratic process. First past the post. No good whinging like a Lib Dem when you lose.

DEBBIE (*resigned*) Well, at least can we have some decent music next week?

JEAN (*condescending*) We'll see, dear. I'm not unreasonable and we may be able to reach a compromise. I believe I have some Frank Sinatra at home. Let's just leave it for now shall we? I suggest we skip the exercises this week to save further unpleasantness and punishment to Betty. Now . . . have we all brought our item of fruit?

(ANNE, DEBBIE *and* IRENE *all sit.* LOUISE *is about to sit down but the spare chair gets used by* MARJ *to rest her bag on, so* LOUISE *remains standing, uncertain what she should do. They all rummage in their bags with the exception of* IRENE *and* LOUISE.)

Obviously you haven't, Louise, but it's a little incentive for us. Whoever loses the most weight in the week wins the fruit.

(JEAN *moves along the line collecting the fruit.*)

That's a very nice peach, Marjorie.

MARJ (*pleased*) It's from my corner shop. 'E's very good, 'is fruit's always nice.

EDNA Always nice.

JEAN (*stopping at* IRENE) Forgotten again, Irene? Fine of twenty pence then, please.

IRENE (*giving* JEAN *the money*) I didn't forget. It looked so tempting on the way here that I ate it.

(JEAN *looks to heaven then returns to the table.*)

JEAN Who's going to be first then? (*Consulting her notes.*) Come along, Debbie, you I think.

DEBBIE (*rising and moving to* JEAN) You're just getting at me because of the exercises! I always dread this bit!

JEAN So do the scales I should think.

(JEAN *places the scales on the floor and* DEBBIE *steps sheepishly on.*)

Right . . . let's see. Oh . . . well done, Debbie . . . marvellous! One pound off. Excellent work. (*Genuinely pleased.*) A few more weeks like that and we'll soon have you back down to your original starting weight.

(DEBBIE *returns to her seat as the others applaud.*)

MARJ (*moving to the scales*) I'll go next. I can never relax 'til I've 'ad me weigh in.

EDNA 'Ad 'er weigh in.

JEAN (*reading the scales*) Oh no! Marjorie . . . ten pounds on!

MARJ Ten pounds . . . an' I've been ever so good!

JEAN (*sadly*) The scales don't lie I'm afraid.

MARJ 'Ere, I've still got me coat on. (*Removing her coat.*) I must be going daft. 'Ow's that?

JEAN Four pounds on.

MARJ 'Ang on . . . (*Taking off her watch.*) Any better?

JEAN Still four pounds.

MARJ (*returning to her chair*) Oh well, never mind . . . it's better than ten isn't it?

JEAN But it's still weight on!

MARJ (*sitting*) But I feel 'appier about it . . . in me own mind.

(JEAN *"tuts" loudly and makes a note in her records.*)

EDNA (*leaning towards* MARJ) But you always keep 'yer coat. on!

MARJ (*grinning slyly at* EDNA) But she doesn't know that.

JEAN (*without looking up from her notes*) I do actually, Marjorie. You next please, Edna.

EDNA Don't worry about me, Mrs L, I won't bother.

JEAN Pardon?

EDNA I won't bother, love. It 'asn't been one of me better weeks.

JEAN I'm afraid it isn't optional, Edna.

EDNA Just put me down for a couple of pounds then . . . that'll do me.

JEAN (*raising her eyes to heaven, then making an entry in her notes*) Irene.

IRENE (*innocent*) Yes?

JEAN On the scales, please. Thank you so much.

(*As* IRENE *moves slowly and reluctantly to the scales,* JEAN *notices that* LOUISE *is still standing.*)

(*to* LOUISE) You're standing again, dear. Do you prefer to stand?

LOUISE Well, I would have sat but . . . (*Pointing vaguely at* MARJ's *bag on the spare chair.*) . . . (*Losing her nerve.*) . . . but I prefer standing . . . very much so . . . very much.

IRENE (*stepping onto the scales*) I feel I must warn you, Jean, I looked at a chocolate gateaux on Saturday and put at least a stone on.

JEAN Well, we'll soon see, won't we, dear. (*Looking at the scales, then at her notes, then back at the scales in disbelief. Sternly.*) Five pounds on.

IRENE I did warn you!

ANNE Five? Five!

(ANNE *starts snorting like a pig. They all join in except* JEAN *and* LOUISE.)

JEAN (*consulting her records*) I don't understand it! There's a pattern, Irene, a definite pattern.

ANNE It's called getting fat.

JEAN You lose weight, then you gain it. Week in, week out . . . you alternate! I've never seen anything like it.

EDNA Alternate.

IRENE It's going to my no-smoking class . . . that's what's doing it.

JEAN What do you mean?

ANNE She's started eating cigarettes instead of smoking them.

IRENE Look, I like coming here, and I like going to the no-smoking class.

BETTY Men.

JEAN But why this pattern?

IRENE Well, if I kept piling weight on *all* the time, you'd kick me out wouldn't you!

JEAN Well, I wouldn't put it quite like that, dear. Obviously we would have to reconsider your position.

EDNA Reconsider.

(JEAN *glares at* EDNA *in irritation.*)

IRENE But the other group think I should be committed to stopping smoking . . . but I can't do both. I stop smoking for a week, which makes me eat, which makes them very happy but upsets you. So, the following week I smoke, but stop eating. It's a vicious circle.

JEAN (*genuinely concerned*) Oh dear . . . oh dear, oh dear.

ANNE — Oh dear, oh dear, oh dear.

EDNA — Oh dear.

JEAN — (*scowling at* ANNE *and* EDNA *in turn*) It seems to me, Irene, that you must make a choice . . . one or the other. We can't have you wandering through no-man's land.

IRENE — Oh, I wouldn't like that . . . no men!

JEAN — I'm trying to be serious, dear!

MARJ — You want to chew gum . . . that's what did the trick wi' me.

EDNA — Gum.

MARJ — I stopped smoking four years ago. 'Ad exactly your trouble. Piled weight on I did.

EDNA — Like an enormous football she was. Awful.

MARJ — (*hurt*) You've never said that! You used to say it looked all right on me!

EDNA — Well, I didn't want to upset you, Marj . . . I knew 'ow 'ard you were trying with your ciggies.

MARJ — Even so . . . you could 'ave said! Anyway, I tried chewing gum. 'Ardly a minute went past without me chewing.

IRENE — And it worked?

MARJ — Me weight, fell off me . . . it fell off!

EDNA Fell off.

BETTY There you are, Irene . . . problem solved.

MARJ I lost most of me teeth, mind.

EDNA With all the chewing.

MARJ I think they were already on their way out though.

EDNA Just 'astened their departure.

MARJ (*thinking deeply*) Come to think of it, that might be what did the trick with me weight. I could 'ardly eat for weeks with me new teeth.

IRENE Oh . . . great!

DEBBIE It's a small price to pay, Irene . . . just go and have all your teeth out.

LOUISE (*helpfully*) My Malcolm's a dentist.

IRENE Well, it's all right, Louise . . . I shan't be troubling him.

LOUISE (*seriously*) Oh, it wouldn't be any trouble . . . it's his job.

(*They all look at* LOUISE *and she realizes it was a silly comment. She smiles, embarrassed.*)

BETTY I couldn't do that job for anything. Spending all day peering into people's mouths.

LOUISE (*trying to redeem herself*) Oh no, Malcolm says it's fascinating . . . he's always talking about it.

ANNE A real wow at parties, I bet.

LOUISE Oh yes . . . he is. Not that we go to an awful lot.

IRENE I wonder why.

JEAN (*quickly*) I think we should move on. Bear my comments in mind, Irene. Betty next I think, thank you.

BETTY I suppose it had to come eventually.

(BETTY *tries to stand but can only do so bent double, groaning and holding her back.*)

Sorry, Jean. I don't think I can make it.

IRENE Debbie . . . look what you've done. Maimed for life!

DEBBIE There's nothing wrong with her! It's just an excuse to stay out of Jean's clutches.

BETTY As if I'd stoop so low.

DEBBIE You couldn't stoop any lower!

BETTY Very funny. (*Sinking back into her chair.*) Sorry, Jean.

JEAN It's all right, Betty. We don't want you straining anything else. We'll just use an estimated weight. I'll put you down for the same as last week.

(*As* JEAN *looks down to fill in her sheet,* BETTY *raises her hands in a gesture of triumph.*)

IRENE — You little rat! I must remember that one for next week.

BETTY — Actually, Jean, I've had a really good week. Lost about half a stone. I'll take the fruit now if you like.

JEAN — Don't worry, dear, if you've lost that much it will show up next week, won't it?

IRENE — Estimated gas meter readings always turn out to be too low as well.

JEAN — (*briskly*) You next please, Anne.

IRENE — Oh goody. I'm expecting a lot from you . . . after your helpful little comments earlier.

ANNE — You won't be disappointed.

(*As* ANNE *steps onto the scales, she tries to keep one foot resting very slightly on the floor.* JEAN *reads the scales without noticing.*)

JEAN — That really is excellent, Anne dear, remarkable . . . Six pounds off!

IRENE — Excuse me, Miss . . . her foot's on the floor.

ANNE — No it isn't.

(ANNE *pulls her foot quickly off the floor. Almost immediately she steps off the scales, but* JEAN *is too quick for her.*)

JEAN Two pounds on. Thank you, Irene.

ANNE (*returning to her chair, to* IRENE) Creep.

JEAN (*consulting her notes*) So . . . let's have a look. That makes Debbie the winner of the fruit with a weight loss of one pound.

(*The rest start to applaud, congratulating* DEBBIE.)

(*cutting*) Which doesn't say much for the rest of you!

(*They all stop applauding, looking guilty.*)

Now then, Louise, we need to get you started, dear. Would you hop on the scales for me and we'll compute your details.

(LOUISE *gets on the scales hesitantly and* JEAN *reads her weight.*)

And what's your height?

LOUISE I think I'm about (*Insert height of actress.*)

JEAN Thank you, dear. You may sit down now . . . or stand if you prefer.

(LOUISE *gets off the scales and stands by, awkwardly as* JEAN *refers to a small handbook.*)

We'll just have to consult the oracle.

DEBBIE Moment of truth, Louise.

IRENE Yes, you'll soon find out what your debauched lifestyle has done to you.

LOUISE (*worried*) Debauched?

JEAN Oh dear. How much did you say you wanted to lose, Louise?

LOUISE My Malcolm thought about a stone and a half.

JEAN Mmm. Out of the question, dear I'm afraid. According to this you're already well within the recommended limits.

LOUISE But I can't be!

JEAN The oracle never lies . . . sorry.

LOUISE But I can't go home and tell Malcolm that! You must be wrong. (*Hopefully.*) Maybe I'm shorter than I thought.

IRENE Not so much over-weight as under-tall.

LOUISE He'll never understand.

BETTY Surely it can't be that bad, Louise?

LOUISE (*tearful*) You don't know him. He says that I'm fat and ugly. He'll leave me . . . I know he will.

JEAN Surely not. You really must pull yourself together, dear . . . you really must try.

ANNE It's disgusting, him getting her in this state.

BETTY Louise . . . has he actually *said* that he would leave you?

LOUISE (*sobbing almost uncontrollably*) Who?

BETTY Malcolm of course.

(*At the name, "Malcolm",* LOUISE *sobs even louder.*)

Has he?

LOUISE Yes . . . well, not exactly . . . but he will . . . I know.

BETTY Well, has he actually said that he thinks you're ugly?

LOUISE He does . . . I can tell.

BETTY But he hasn't actually said so? So what *did* he say . . . exactly?

LOUISE He said I should come to a slimming club. So he must think I'm fat and ugly.

BETTY He just said that . . . out of the blue . . . that you've got to slim?

LOUISE Yes . . . practically.

BETTY How do you mean, practically?

LOUISE Well, I said to him . . . I said, "Malcolm, do you think I'm getting fat?", and he didn't say anything.

BETTY So?

LOUISE So then I said, "Do you think I should go to a slimming club", and he still just kept quiet . . . you know, like he didn't want to tell me how awful I looked.

BETTY But he still didn't say anything?

LOUISE But then I asked him again, "Malcolm, am I fat and ugly". And do you know what he said? He said "yes" . . . just like that . . . he just looked up from his paper and grunted at me.

IRENE I could tell mine I was having a passionate affair with the milkman. If he was in the middle of his paper *he'd* just grunt at me.

MARJ My Arthur's like that. It's very 'andy really 'cos I get all sorts out of 'im when 'e's not listening.

EDNA All sorts.

MARJ Serves 'im right . . . ignorant pig!

BETTY Louise, did he actually say a stone and a half?

LOUISE No . . . but he agreed with me.

IRENE While he was still reading the paper?

LOUISE No this was much later . . . when he was watching the snooker.

IRENE That's it then. He's probably sat at home right now, wondering where you are! He won't have a clue.

LOUISE No, he knows I've come. He was at home, cleaning his car cleaning machine.

BETTY Look, love, if you'll take my advice, just go home and forget about the whole thing.

LOUISE But I told him I was coming here. He always says I'm indecisive and never follow things through properly. Besides, I want him to see that I'm making an effort for him. That's important in a marriage isn't it . . . making an effort.

IRENE No . . . most men think it's important for the *woman* to make an effort. *They* never bother though.

JEAN I'm afraid none of this makes a difference. The fact is, Louise, that I can't condone you losing weight. What if you fell ill? I'd never forgive myself . . . I'd be castigated by the club.

EDNA Castigated.

DEBBIE It would make a change. You usually get told off for building us up!

JEAN Which brings me conveniently to my next point. I have received another letter.

IRENE Watch out, girls, slapped wrists time.

JEAN I would appreciate it if we could treat the matter with appropriate gravity.

IRENE (*helpfully*) Without gravity we wouldn't weigh anything.

(JEAN *glares at her.*)

Sorry, just a thought.

JEAN (*picking up a letter from the table*) I think it best if I simply read directly from the key areas. (*Reading*) "Dear Mrs Laverick" . . . etcetera, etcetera . . . "we note from your records that, over the past four months, the total weight gain of your members amounts to three stones thirteen pounds. Despite previous reminders" . . . etcetera . . . "regrettable situation" . . . etcetera . . . "and we must inform you that, unless an immediate and dramatic improvement takes place, we will have no option other than to request your resignation as branch organiser. If no suitable replacement were to be found, the branch would have to be closed" . . . etcetera, etcetera . . . "yours sincerely" . . . etcetera.

EDNA Etcetera.

IRENE It's to the point anyway.

ANNE So what if they do sling us out! It doesn't bother me. We could still meet couldn't we?

JEAN But it bothers me, Anne. It bothers me deeply. It's my responsibility. Quite frankly . . . I feel ashamed . . . deeply ashamed.

(*She breaks off dramatically, voice shaking. There is an embarrassed silence for several seconds.*)

MARJ Does anybody fancy taking over then?

(JEAN *glances sharply at* MARJ, *deeply hurt.*)

(*trying to redeem herself*) Well, don't you worry yourself, Mrs L, we'll all just 'ave to try 'arder.

EDNA 'Arder.

BETTY Perhaps we've just lost our motivation. Maybe if we all talked about why we're here, we could make a determined new start.

JEAN I hardly think talk will help. One hesitates to mention it but the crux of the whole matter is that you must all eat less!

(*They all look stunned.*)

IRENE But Betty's right. Perhaps we've lost track of why we're doing it. I mean, let's try it . . . why do you come here, Betty?

(*Throughout the following conversations,* ANNE *becomes increasingly agitated.*)

BETTY (*thoughtfully, after some hesitation*) I suppose it's since I lost Doug. I don't get out very much to meet people socially. At first that didn't matter, but it reached a stage where it did. I thought slimming would be a start of a new life . . . a new me, if you like . . . to give me more confidence . . . maybe even find a little romance.

JEAN (*taking renewed interest*) What about you, Debbie?

DEBBIE Oh . . . a mixture of things really. Clothes I suppose . . . I want to wear exactly what I want and look good in them. And Wayne . . . I want to look good for him. I just like eating too much. I will make an effort though . . . from now on.

MARJ — And so will I, Mrs L. I'd 'ate to see you 'umiliated because of us!

JEAN — A very noble sentiment, Marj, but can you really do it? In fairness, it hasn't gone well to date.

MARJ — You can depend on me, Mrs L. I'll just tell my Arthur straight . . . Mrs L's 'ole reputation depends on me. I'll sort 'im out.

JEAN — But it's *you* who's supposed to be losing the weight, not Arthur.

MARJ — But it's 'is fault I don't! 'E likes a bit o' meat on a woman, as he puts it. 'Ates 'em too scraggy.

EDNA — 'Ates it.

MARJ — 'E looks at me sometimes and 'e says; "just look at you; wasting away to nothing you are". But don't you worry, Mrs L, I'll tell 'im.

JEAN — (*genuinely touched*) Well, thank you, Marjorie . . . thank you very much. What about you, Edna?

EDNA — I'm with 'er.

JEAN — You mean you share her sentiments?

EDNA — No . . . I mean I'm with 'er. I come 'ere with 'er.

JEAN — But what about slimming?

EDNA — Oh, I'm not interested in that. It's just a bit of a night out. Then on the way 'ome we stop off and 'ave a glass o' stout (MARJ *glares at her.*) . . . and then we get some fish and chips from the corner.

(MARJ *nudges her fiercely.* EDNA *looks puzzled for a second, then catches on.*)

What? Oh . . . er . . . we don't often 'ave a stout mind . . . or chips . . . just a bit 'o fish . . . with no batter.

JEAN — Thank you so much, Edna. I think we get the picture.

IRENE — I want to be sexy.

JEAN — Good, yes . . . go on.

IRENE — Isn't that enough!

JEAN — Well . . . I was just expecting a little more, that's all.

IRENE — There isn't any more.

JEAN — Right . . . good. Anne?

ANNE — (*fuming*) It's pathetic isn't it!

IRENE — Are you talking about me!

ANNE — All of you . . . it's pathetic! Can't you see what you're doing!

IRENE — I'm sure you're going to tell us.

ANNE Everyone of you . . . men. If they tell you to slim, you slim. If they tell you not to slim, you don't. Why don't you decide for yourselves? Why don't you tell them where they can go? Men rule your lives!

EDNA They don't rule mine . . . I'm with 'er.

ANNE (*ignoring her*) Aren't you allowed to think for yourselves! Do you have to do everything to please *them*?

IRENE There's nothing wrong with wanting to look attractive. Even *you* might scrub up quite well if you made an effort!

ANNE But you should think for yourselves!

BETTY Anne, calm down. You shouldn't have said that, Irene.

IRENE (*to* ANNE) Okay then, Mrs High and Mighty. Why do you come here? Tell us . . . why?

(ANNE *suddenly looks very uncertain of herself.*)

LOUISE (*who is now looking very uncomfortable*) I really think I ought to be getting off. (*Standing.*) It's been very nice thank you.

IRENE You're not going anywhere, Louise. And for goodness sake, sit down will you?

LOUISE (*meekly*) Oh, all right then.

(LOUISE *moves to sit and* MARJ *obligingly moves her bag off the chair to make space. As* LOUISE *sits,* MARJ *smiles encouragingly at her.*)

IRENE Anne was just about to enlighten us.

BETTY I think we should just leave it.

IRENE Why should we? She started it! Why is she here?

ANNE It's nothing to do with you.

IRENE No, come on . . . why are you here, Anne? We're all just dying to know.

ANNE Just leave me alone will you.

IRENE But you shouldn't start things you can't finish!

ANNE Just leave me! (*Jumping up and running out of the door screaming.*) Leave me alone!

JEAN (*following* ANNE *to the door*) Anne . . . Anne, dear?

BETTY (*quietly*) It's all right, Jean. Best just to leave her. I'll call in on her later. Well done, Irene!

IRENE She started it!

BETTY But you don't understand.

IRENE I was only asking her! There was no need for her to go dashing off like that.

BETTY — You know her husband left her a couple of years ago?

IRENE — I'm not surprised if she carries on like that!

BETTY — He went off with a very slim, very attractive woman, without any warning at all. Anne's convinced he walked out on her because she was fat. She isn't of course, but try telling her that. It's an obsession.

DEBBIE — That's why she's so anti-men?

LOUISE — How awful. It must be dreadful to be paranoid like that!

IRENE — Well, how was I supposed to know? It's not my fault.

BETTY — I know, but you are a bit like a bull in a china shop when you start.

LOUISE — (*worried*) What if I become paranoid! What would Malcolm think of me then! Do you think Malcolm thinks I'm paranoid?

JEAN — Louise, pull yourself together, please. We have enough on our plate at the moment . . . thank you so much.

EDNA — On our plate.

IRENE — I feel dreadful. Do you think she'll ever come back after that episode?

BETTY — Oh, I'll talk her round. She'll be back next week.

JEAN — But will we still be in existence next week?

DEBBIE Of course we will.

JEAN I wish I were able to share your optimism.

DEBBIE But it's easy. I've just thought of the perfect solution. Look, we've got a slimming club that insists, for some reason or other, that we lose weight.

JEAN Therein lies the problem.

DEBBIE But we also have Louise who is paranoid about her weight.

EDNA Paranoid.

(LOUISE *looks at* DEBBIE *in alarm.*)

DEBBIE (*quickly*) Did I say paranoid? I didn't mean that, Louise, honestly. All I meant was that you don't really need to lose any weight . . . scientifically speaking.

JEAN Sorry, dear . . . don't follow.

DEBBIE Let Louise join . . . then slightly misread her weight . . . by a couple of stones. You can gradually correct your mistake over the next few months.

JEAN But that is dishonest, Debbie!

DEBBIE Course it is. It's also brilliant. Louise proves to her husband that she's really making a decisive effort by joining a slimming club and we look good because she'll be our best slimmer ever.

JEAN I'm sorry, Debbie, it's unthinkable.

DEBBIE And when we look good, Jean . . . you'll look good.

JEAN Will I?

DEBBIE Of course. And Louise wouldn't mind, would you?

LOUISE Well, I don't know. I suppose I wouldn't actually have to lie to Malcolm, would I? I'd just say I'd joined a slimming club.

(JEAN *considers the idea for a few seconds, warming to the prospect of appearing to run a successful club.*)

JEAN I wonder if you might just pop back onto the scales, Louise. I seem to have mislaid my note of your weight.

(LOUISE *moves to stand on the scales.*)

Let's have a look then, dear. (*Shaking her head.*) The light in here really is dreadful, you know. Oh dear, Louise, look at this . . . five stones overweight.

BETTY Five!

JEAN May as well be hung for a sheep as a lamb.

IRENE You're too good at this . . . I bet you've done it before.

JEAN (*innocently*) Done what, dear? Thank you, Louise. I suppose I should outline the diet plan to you, but in your particular case, I suggest you eat whatever you like. Right, shall we get these things cleared away. Perhaps you'd give me a hand Debbie, thank you so much.

(JEAN *and* DEBBIE *begin to clear the chairs to the back of the room as the others get ready to leave.* BETTY *shows no sign of her back problem.*)

IRENE — I see your back's improved, Betty.

BETTY — Oh, yes. With all the excitement I'd forgotten about it.

IRENE — I knew it was a con!

BETTY — You seem to have a very low opinion of me, Irene.

IRENE — On the contrary . . . you got away with it.

MARJ — Right then, Ed . . . we'll get off for our stou . . . (*Noticing that* JEAN *is close enough to hear.*) stroll 'ome.

(JEAN *smiles to herself, satisfied.*)

EDNA — (*not realizing that* JEAN *is close behind*) And I'm going to be very good with the chips tonight.

(JEAN'S *smile becomes broader.*)

I'll just 'ave the *one* 'elping o' mushy peas with 'em.

(JEAN'S *smile turns to a scowl.* MARJ *and* EDNA *move towards the door.* IRENE *calls after them in a loud whisper.* JEAN *moves further away as she stacks another chair but is obviously listening.*)

IRENE — You two still all right for Friday?

MARJ — Wouldn't miss it . . . see you then. Ta ta all.

EDNA — Ta ta all.

(*There is a chorus of goodbyes as* MARJ *and* EDNA *exit.* IRENE *draws* LOUISE *to one side.*)

IRENE — Are you interested in coming to our little binge on Friday?

LOUISE — Binge?

IRENE — We have one every fortnight . . . we all go out for a meal and have a massive blow-out.

LOUISE — Oh . . . well I don't know about . . .

IRENE — Come on, you'd enjoy it. You don't even have to worry about the consequences either. You're going to lose five stones over the next few months whether you like it or not!

LOUISE — But it's Malcolm . . . I'm not sure what he'd say. It does sound rather good fun though. Perhaps I will . . . if he's out at his golf club.

IRENE — Good. (*To* BETTY.) Louise is going to join us on Friday. (*To* LOUISE.) Seven o'clock, outside the post office.

LOUISE Oh . . . but it's not definite.

BETTY Yes it is . . . we'll pick you up. I think we should have a change of venue though. Do you fancy the Italian this week?

IRENE Why there?

BETTY I'll make sure Anne comes along. I think it will do her a lot of good.

IRENE All that pasta!

BETTY Just something I found out recently. The woman her husband went off with works in there. She started about a year ago . . . the food apparently seems to have got the better of her.

IRENE The slim one?

BETTY I'm reliably informed that she now looks like a Bulgarian shot putter. I think Anne might enjoy herself.

(JEAN *and* DEBBIE *have finished with the chairs.* DEBBIE *moves to the others as* JEAN *clears things from the table into her bag.*)

Fancy a quick drink with Marj and Edna.

IRENE Why not. You coming, Deb?

DEBBIE Disco. See you Friday though.

(IRENE, BETTY *and* LOUISE *move to the door as* DEBBIE *starts to put her coat on.*)

BETTY Bye, Jean. Promise we'll all be trying our best for you.

JEAN I do hope so, dear . . . I do hope so.

(IRENE, BETTY *and* LOUISE *exit to a chorus of farewells.* JEAN *finishes packing her things and intercepts* DEBBIE *as she moves towards the door.*)

I must admit, Debbie, that idea of yours was marvellous.

DEBBIE I do have them sometimes. Not as stupid as I look.

JEAN Tell me, dear. What was all of that about Friday? I couldn't help overhearing.

DEBBIE (*in panic*) Oh . . . er . . . Friday?

JEAN Yes, dear, Friday. It regularly follows Thursday.

DEBBIE Oh, we're just going out . . . a few of us . . . for a change.

JEAN Lovely. Anywhere interesting?

DEBBIE Interesting? Oh no . . . shouldn't think so. Theatre I would think . . . or somewhere . . . similar.

JEAN Oh, I do so love the theatre. Do you have tickets?

DEBBIE No, yes . . . no, I don't think so. We're going on spec I think.

JEAN Then I may just join you. I'm sure the girls wouldn't mind, would they?

DEBBIE Mind? Course not . . . no. Why should they?

JEAN Seven o'clock at the post office I believe. I'll look forward to it.

DEBBIE Yeah . . . whatever. (*Moving towards the door.*) Goodnight then.

JEAN Goodnight. Oh, just one thing. I will try *very* hard to be there for seven, but you will all hang on if I happen to be a few minutes late? It's rather a difficult time for me and . . . oh, but there's no need for me to explain is there, dear . . . what's a few minutes between friends?

DEBBIE (*weakly*) Yeah . . . exactly. We'll see you then.

JEAN So looking forward to it.

(DEBBIE *exits looking very deflated.* JEAN *looks very pleased with herself, picks up her things and moves to the door.*)

(*to herself as she turns to check that the room is clear*) Yes . . . I'll look forward to it very much. I think we may just be getting somewhere at last.

(JEAN *smiles to herself and exits as the curtain falls.*)

PROPERTY LIST

Set
- Stack of 8 chairs
- Small table
- Several cardboard boxes; one containing cardboard cut-out skull
- No smoking sign
- Shopping bag containing bathroom scales, portable CD player, folders, handbook, notes, letter, paper, pens and pencils
- Other items and notices to suggest a well-used Church Hall

Offstage

Personal
- Wrist watch (JEAN)
- Bag containing piece of fruit (BETTY)
- Bag containing piece of fruit (ANNE)
- Bag containing packet of cigarettes, twenty pence (IRENE)
- Bag containing packet of cigarettes, CD, piece of fruit (DEBBIE)
- Handbag containing (LOUISE)
- Wrist watch, bag containing a peach (MARJORIE)
- Bag containing piece of fruit (EDNA)

EFFECTS PLOT

Cue 1 Jean: ". . . A one, a two, a one two three four . . ." Page 17.
'Sing-along' music starts.

Cue 2 Debbie: "Oh, this is impossible." Page 19.
Music stops.

Cue 3 Irene: "Oh, get a life, Jean." Page 20.
Disco music starts.

Cue 4 Irene: "Are you all right, Betty?" Page 21.
Music stops.